Original title:
A Whisper from the Ocean

Copyright © 2025 Creative Arts Management OÜ
All rights reserved.

Author: Rafael Sterling
ISBN HARDBACK: 978-1-80581-692-8
ISBN PAPERBACK: 978-1-80581-219-7
ISBN EBOOK: 978-1-80581-692-8

Whispered Travels of the Ocean's Heart

Tiny turtles dance with glee,
Shells clattering like a grand spree.
Starfish try to tell a joke,
But seaweed laughs 'til it chokes.

Crabs in tuxedos strut with style,
Sandy beaches—it's their aisle.
Fish in bow ties swim around,
Making sure their party's loud.

Dolphins dive and do a flip,
Sipping seawater from a cup.
They send bubbles up with flair,
To tickle mermaids—what a scare!

With every wave that rolls and dips,
Giggles echo from little fish lips.
Anemones wave with all their might,
In this ocean of pure delight!

Melodies in Distant Waters

Sailing boats with parrots squawking,
While crabs play drums—they're not talking!
Seagulls join in with a caw,
As fish all dance without a flaw.

Octopus conducts with flair and grace,
Shells join in for a singing race.
As waves clink like glasses of cheer,
A party starts, so bring your beer!

Jellyfish float in a wobbly beat,
Their glow lights up like a disco feat.
Clams open wide for a good laugh,
Making jokes on their pearl-studded bath.

So come, my friends, to the briny blue,
Where laughter and joy are waiting for you.
With every splash a new tale begins,
Come join us; let's see who wins!

Lapping Lullabies

The waves gently giggle, tickling the shore,
Crabs hold a dance-off, what a wild score!
Starfish doing ballet, clams play the drums,
Even the dolphins are cracking up, here comes the fun!

The seagulls are squawking, with poor timing too,
They're offbeat with laughter, still, that's nothing new.
The sandcastles tumble, but who needs a crown?
When the ocean is laughing, you can't wear a frown!

A Symphony of Seabeds

Listen closely to the conch, it hums a tune,
While squids throw a party under the moon.
Octopus conductor waves his arms in flair,
Shells play the maracas, what a wild affair!

The jellyfish jiggle, floating with style,
Turtles tap dance, they'll entertain for a while.
Anemones swaying, grinning wide with glee,
Making music all night, oh, what jubilee!

Waterscapes of Longing

The fish peek above, playing hide and seek,
With bubbles as giggles, they're quite the cheek!
Mermaids trade gossip, tossing seaweed with flair,
As waves dance in rhythm, without a single care.

Seashells are blushing, they gossip all day,
About the romantic crabs who'd dance and sway.
Whales share bad jokes, with big belly laughs,
Every splash telling tales of oceanic gaffs!

Shadows in the Surf

The surfers are tumbling, what a funny sight,
Wipeouts are the norm, they're a comical plight.
Shadows dart underwater; fish make a race,
Jellyfish just giggle, taking their place.

Sea turtles are watching, hands on their cheeks,
As barnacles crack jokes about those weird peaks.
Now everyone's swimming, but who's got the style?
The ocean's full of laughter, wave after wave, mile after mile!

Songs from the Seafoam

Bubbles sing a silly tune,
Fish dance under the moon.
Crabs in hats, they stomp and cheer,
Splashing joy from ear to ear.

Seagulls squawk with laughter loud,
Waving wings, they form a crowd.
Jellyfish wear their finest ties,
Tickling waves with goofy sighs.

Currents of Serenity

The starfish plays a ukulele,
While clams join in, oh-so-saily.
Octopus conducts with great delight,
As dolphins spin in pure moonlight.

Turtles race in flip-flop shoes,
Singing blues with splashes and hues.
The seaweed sways, a laughing band,
Joking tides that tickle the sand.

Echoes of the Tides

Waves crash loud, they tell a joke,
Salty air, a merry smoke.
Seashells giggle on the shore,
As crabs tell tales of ocean lore.

Starfish wink with glittery eyes,
Flipping tales of silly lies.
The moon above joins in the fun,
Shining bright 'til day is done.

Secrets Beneath the Waves

Underneath, a party brews,
Mermaids spread the gossip news.
Eels in bowties twist and twirl,
While sea cucumbers dance and whirl.

Waves conspire with barnacle friends,
Laughter echoes, never ends.
The treasure chest grins wide and glee,
For secrets whispered joyfully.

Cries of the Distant Shore

The seagulls caw, with quite a flair,
They steal my chips without a care.
The waves crash in, they start to dance,
While crabs just plot their crabby advance.

The lifeguard shouts, he's lost his hat,
And there's a dolphin, oh look at that!
It jumps and squeaks, as if to say,
'Stop feeding me fries, I'm on a spray!'

The Sea's Hidden Voice

Under the surface, bubbles float,
A fish called Fred sings out a note.
He sings of love and other gaffes,
While wearing seaweed as his scarves.

The octopus plays the saxophone,
In a jazzy tune, he's all alone.
With eight long arms, he plays with glee,
Requesting songs from the deep blue sea!

Submerged Stories

Each tide brings tales from far away,
Of mermaids giggling and sharks at play.
They ride the waves on boards made of kelp,
Exchanging secrets the sea creatures help.

A crab in sunglasses flicks, 'Look at me!'
While plankton party with frenzied glee.
They dance in circles, a swirling bowl,
While whales share jokes, they're very droll!

Melodies of the Deep Blue

The conch shell hums a silly tune,
While turtles surf beneath the moon.
A clam is pranking, hiding its pearl,
While sea stars giggle in a whirl.

"Watch my flip!" a fish doth shout,
But belly-flops leave him in doubt.
With a flick and a splash, he makes a fuss,
As dolphins laugh, "Come join the bus!"

Waters that Hold Forgotten Prayers

In blue depths where fish wear suits,
The seaweed dances, wearing boots.
Starfish hold meetings, it's quite a sight,
They argue about who glows more bright.

Conch shells gossip, they can't keep still,
About a crab who climbed up a hill.
The tides laugh loudly, waves spill tea,
As mermaids tease fish, all in good glee.

Glistening Hopes at Dusk

Seashells chatter on the golden shore,
Jellyfish giggle, they float, then they soar.
Seagulls in sunglasses, oh what a sight,
They squawk over popcorn, a snack for the night.

The stars wink down, like cheeky old friends,
As sandcastles plot how the sea bends.
With buckets and spades, pirates unite,
Deciding which treasure to steal for tonight.

The Heartbeat of the Abyss

Octopuses dance wearing polka dot ties,
They twist and they twirl, oh my, what a guise!
The jellyfish float, all covered in gleam,
While clams complain, 'Life's not as it seems.'

Sharks in tuxedos swim by with a grin,
While lobsters debate who wears the best skin.
The coral reefs chuckle, so bright and so bold,
Reciting old tales that never get old.

Cries of the Untamed Coast

Dolphins play tag, they leap with pure joy,
They giggle and splash like a cheeky toy.
Walruses lounge, putting on a grand show,
Discussing the weather while munching on snow.

The wind sings a tune full of playful spree,
As crabs host a party beneath the sea.
With laughter and smiles, they splash all about,
In this funny world, there's never a doubt.

Dance of the Flickering Lanternfish

In the depths where shadows play,
Tiny fish light up the bay.
They twirl and twist in a glow,
Making seashells tap to and fro.

With a flash and a cheeky grin,
They tease the crabs to jump in.
"Come on, join our sparkling spree!"
"You've got shells, just follow me!"

Flipping back, they giggle loud,
Casting sparks, an underwater crowd.
Even eels start to groove,
Finding their rhythm, they bust a move!

When morning comes, they take a bow,
"See you tonight, we'll wow the crowd!"
With winks and bubbles, they depart,
Left behind, a giddy heart.

The Ocean's Breath in Midnight Air

Under the stars, the ocean sighs,
Sending laughs in slippery ties.
A crab writes poetry on the sand,
While starfish clap with all they planned.

Seashells gossip, oh what a sight!
"Did you see that wave? It took a flight!"
With puffy fish warning, "Watch your back!"
As barnacles giggle, not a crack!

The moon's reflection makes waves giggle,
As dolphins join in, sharing a fiddle.
They leap and splash, what a bold show,
Spraying water like a circus pro!

The night unfolds with quirky tales,
Of underwater ships and whale's wails.
And as dawn breaks, a bright new day,
The ocean's jokes will never sway.

Traces of Magic in the Mists

Fog rolls in with a playful tease,
As sea otters float with the breeze.
They juggle kelp with shiny rocks,
Crafting laughter in little knocks.

A seagull squawks, "I'm the best!
Watch me dive, I'm on a quest!"
But with a flop and a splashy sound,
He flips right over, floundering around!

Mermaids giggle from reefs so bright,
"Your somersault's a comical sight!"
With snapper fish rolling their eyes,
"Oh, take the plunge, don't be shy!"

As the mists clear, they cheer and clap,
Sharing secrets in a fishy map.
The magic's there, all fun and free,
In the ocean's heart, where spirits spree.

Fables of the Gull's Flight

A gull with dreams of soaring high,
Decided one day to touch the sky.
With a flap and a clumsy spin,
He accidentally dove right in!

Caught in bubbles, he puffed out his chest,
"Who knew water would be my best jest?"
With a splash and a laughing cheer,
His pals swooped low to lend an ear.

"Take it easy, flyboy, no need to dive!"
They honked and chortled, so alive.
With feathers ruffled and spirit bright,
They joined in his splashy, silly flight.

Now every gull, with a wink and a grin,
Knows it's okay to take a spin.
And if they plunge, oh what a sight,
Just rise again, turn it to light!

Lullabies of the Coastline

The waves laugh softly, tickling the sand,
Seagulls squawking, a comic band.
Shells scatter stories, each one goes by,
With crabs in tuxedos, they strut and high-five.

A beach ball giggles, rolls on the tide,
All the starfish dance, with nowhere to hide.
Flip-flops are flying, lost in the chase,
As kids dodge the sun, sunscreen on their face.

Jellyfish jelly, a delicacy rare,
But those wobbling wonders, just float in despair.
A sandcastle throne for a daydreaming queen,
With a crown made of seaweed, fit for a scene.

So evenings approach with the sun's big farewell,
The tide tells tall tales that only we tell.
Laughing with dolphins, we join in the cheer,
As the ocean chuckles, it's music to hear.

The Depths' Gentle Secrets

Under the surface, fish dance in delight,
With bubble-blowing whales, they giggle and bite.
Octopuses juggle in a bright underwater show,
Their antics are pure magic, a watery glow.

Clams have their clamshells, always in pairs,
Telling secrets of treasure, hidden in lairs.
Sea cucumbers grumble, 'We're so underrated!'
While sharks tease sea horses; 'You're so inflated!'

A pirate fish, grumpy, guards his gold stash,
But sea urchins scatter, just hoping to dash.
With starry-eyed crabs in a waltz so divine,
The ocean's own ballet; it's dance time, not dine!

So when you dive deep, don't be in a hurry,
Join in the laughter, don't fret, don't worry.
For the depths hold a comedy, waiting for you,
With friends of all kinds in a whimsical crew.

Chasing Shadows of the Shore

Footprints lead nowhere, like a riddle in sand,
As shadows skip by, doing a strange dance hand in hand.
A clam leads a conga, the barnacles laugh,
As the tide keeps on teasing, it's a playful gaffe.

The sun plays coy, hiding behind a plume,
While crabs break a leg in their crabby costume.
Wave after wave, they call out and sway,
Turning the shoreline into a comical play.

Jellyfish float in like they own the place,
With squishy blubber and a buoyant grace.
Turtles in shades soak up the bright rays,
Snapping selfies with fish in their sun-soaked phase.

As dusk paints the sky with a wink and a nod,
The ocean's alive with a laugh and a prod.
So if you hear chuckles when the tide is in,
It's just the sea giggling, let the fun begin!

Songs of the Distant Barking Seals

Barking seals huddle, a raucous delight,
Their voices a chorus in the soft moonlight.
With flippers a-flapping, they start up the fun,
Rolling and tumbling, oh what a run!

Sea lions lounge with a lazy old grin,
While octopuses play hide-and-seek from within.
A dolphin dips low, brings gifts from the deep,
As starfish cheer on, their secrets to keep.

The evening brings tales of fishy romance,
As squids spin stories with a slippery dance.
With bubbles of laughter, they rise to the top,
A party of critters that never will stop.

So if you should wander by shores of great glee,
Join in the ballet of the wild jubilee.
With each wave that crashes, hear joy in the hail,
For the music keeps playing from barking of seals.

Tides of Secrets

When the waves start to giggle,
Seashells play a prank or two.
Starfish wear silly glasses,
While the crab does a little jiggle.

Seagulls squawk with joyful tunes,
Dolphins dance in swirling arcs.
Anemones turn to balloons,
While the fish make silly quarks.

The currents carry jokes untold,
As the tide rolls in with glee.
The ocean's heart, both brave and bold,
Is a stage for fishy comedy.

With a splash and frolic here and there,
Underneath the sun's bright ray,
Every creature, full of flair,
Has its own part to play.

Echoes Beneath the Waves

Bubbles giggle, rise, and pop,
Echoes of laughter fill the sea.
Octopuses play hopscotch, non-stop,
While sea turtles grow mustaches with glee.

A clam tells fishy tales so tall,
While shrimp paint smiles on their shells,
The jellyfish sway, having a ball,
In their own little world of jolly spells.

Coral reefs gossip all day long,
About who wore the snazziest hues.
The kelp lets out a silly song,
As the flounder shares its latest news.

Surfers ride the waves of cheer,
While the tides mouth secret puns.
The ocean's humor, loud and clear,
Is a treasure for everyone!

Secrets Beneath the Surface

Beneath the waves, where giggles hide,
The fish tell jokes with their fins.
Sea cucumbers join the ride,
While seahorses wear silly grins.

Crabs compete in racing shells,
As shrimp wear party hats so bright.
Clownfish crack the best of spells,
Making the sea a sheer delight.

The oysters play their secret games,
While dolphins make a splashy cheer.
Sardines play tag with crazy names,
In a world where giggles persevere.

A treasure chest of laughter lies,
In the depths where no one sees.
The sea's winks and funny sighs,
Bring joy with every breeze.

Murmurs of the Deep

From the depths, a chuckle flows,
Whales pass notes with silly rhymes.
Grouper fish wear fancy clothes,
While crabs swap jokes in funny climes.

The seaweed sways with a cheeky grin,
As the porpoise cracks a pun.
The starry skies let laughter in,
Bringing joy to everyone.

Barnacles bust out a dance,
While angelfish show off their flair.
The ocean's humor gives a glance,
To life found beneath the air.

With every wave that rolls and sweeps,
A secret giggle drifts along.
In the hearts where laughter peeps,
The ocean sings its cheerful song.

The Lure of Faraway Horizons

The sun laughs loud upon the waves,
Seagulls dance like they're on stage.
A crab wears shades, looking so cool,
While fish flip tricks, breaking every rule.

A pelican drops a fish like a pro,
But missed the hoop, the crowd yells 'Whoa!'
Sandcastles built just to be crushed,
By a sneaky wave, oh how we rushed!

Funky seaweed curls with flair,
It sways and bows without a care.
Shells tell tales, but they're all lies,
"Why did the clam cross the shore?"—surprise!

So raise your glasses, toast the sea,
Where laughter floats, wild and free.
With every wave, a giggle flows,
In salty tales where humor grows.

Lost Voices of the Sea

The dolphins joke, they splash and glide,
While fishes giggle, tongues untied.
A whale sings off-key, full of pride,
He's auditioning for a show—oh, what a ride!

Coral reefs crack jokes in a bright hue,
They're the stand-up comedians, that's true!
An octopus twirls, wearing a hat,
He dances with clams, and they all chat.

Crabby old sailors once gave a frown,
Now they laugh as they flop around.
The seaweed whispers giggles anew,
Tickling the toes of the wandering crew.

Mermaids giggle, tangled in nets,
They tease and play with no regrets.
Lost voices echo in salty breath,
A humorous tune that conquers death.

Reflections in the Waving Grass

Beneath the waves, grass gently sways,
Even the turtles enjoy sunny days.
Tickled by currents, they laugh and dive,
With shells and laughter, they come alive.

Starfish wear glasses, what a sight!
Counting the stars, oh what a night!
A clam yells, "Hey! Keep it down!"
He's trying to nap, but who wears the crown?

The shoreline hums a merry tune,
As jellyfish waltz under the moon.
They're disco kings of the ocean's floor,
In shiny gowns and slippers galore.

So come take a stroll on the sandy path,
Join in the fun, ignore the math.
In nature's humor, we find our bliss,
In grassy reflections, we find our kiss.

The Pulse of the Aquatic Cosmos

Anemones jiggle in the cosmic flow,
Their colors pop—like a wild light show.
A starfish spins, declares he's a star,
With ocean laughter, they travel far.

A clownfish cracks jokes, it's his best part,
Goofy and bright, he's a real sweetheart.
Whales pump up the bass in the swell,
Creating a rhythm, casting a spell.

Kelp forests sway like they're in a trance,
Seahorses twirl, inviting the dance.
Bubble-blowing contests are on display,
As sea turtles cheer with joy all day.

So surf the vibes of this ocean beat,
Where the laughter's rich and the humor's sweet.
In this aquatic realm, let joy explode,
On the pulse of life, let's lighten the load.

Tides of Time and Memory

The waves come crashing, oh what a show,
Reminds me of dancing, with my toes in tow.
Seagulls gossip like they own the sand,
Making mockeries of my beach tan plan.

Shells tell stories, or so they claim,
But all I hear is a game of name.
I asked a crab for some wisdom, you see,
He just pinched me and fled to the sea!

The tides are tricky, they wave hello,
While I'm busy chasing my runaway shoe.
With every retreat, they pull me in tight,
Like an old friend saying, "Stay for the night!"

Yet here I stand, as the sunset gleams,
Tangled in laughter, and sand in my dreams.
A memory made of salt and of fun,
Waved goodbye as the day came undone.

Secrets Minted in the Foam

The ocean's secrets bubble and froth,
I'm convinced they're just gossip like cloth.
A fish tells tales of my last beach fling,
While shells chime in, orchestrating a sing.

Crabs debate fashion, it's quite a sight,
Shells flaunt their colors all day and night.
I tried to join, but was met with a glare,
They whispered, "Human, you haven't a prayer!"

The foam tickles toes like a playful tease,
And seaweed wiggles, if you please.
Each wave that rolls, a giggle it throws,
Like the ocean's own stand-up comedy show.

In this sandy circus, I'm lost in the fun,
While sea critters plot their next marathon run.
With laughter and splashes, I know I will stay,
For in this foamy realm, I'm goofy all day!

Whispers from the Abyss

In the depths they chatter, beneath the waves,
Fish tell tales of the humans they save.
"Look at that fellow, he fell off his raft!"
They giggle together; oh, what a craft!

An octopus argues with a flatfish friend,
"Your swimming's tedious, just twist and pretend!"
He wraps up a rock like a safe little pet,
While clams clap their shells, they're not done yet.

The kelp forest sways, giggling 'neath blue,
With shrimp playing tag, oh what a crew!
A dolphin burst out, with a joke to relay,
"Ever seen a sea lion try to ballet?"

And as I observe, lost in their jest,
I chuckle along, feeling very impressed.
For down in the depths, where the sunlight won't reach,
The laughter runs wild, a magical beach!

Cradle of the Deep Blue

In the cradle below, where the currents swirl,
Fish dream of flying, oh what a pearl!
They gawk at the seagulls, so high in the air,
While I sip my soda, with nary a care.

The jellyfish jive, with a flick and a float,
Making moonlit moves in their sparkling coat.
"Are you lost?" I ask, "Or just drifting along?"
They winked back at me, "We've got it all wrong!"

The dolphins convene, with a splash and a cheer,
They hold a convention; the agenda is clear.
"Today we discuss, the art of the flip,
And which color fish delivers the best quip."

With laughter in layers, the ocean's a ball,
For even in depths, humor isn't so small.
So here I shall stay, in this watery crew,
In the cradle of laughter, the deep shades of blue.

The Rhythm of Rolling Surf

The crabs dance sideways, all out of sync,
While the seagulls squawk, can't find their drink.
Waves crash and giggle, with frothy delight,
As fish play tag in the warm, sunny light.

A starfish named Ted dreamed of being a star,
But his buddies would laugh, 'You won't get far!'
He waved from the sand, 'Hey, don't be so mean!'
As he practiced his moves like a floating marionette queen.

Each tide that rolls in brings secrets untold,
Like clams playing poker, with pearls to unfold.
The seaweed sings softly, a chorus so sweet,
While the dolphins throw parties, now that's quite a feat!

So let's jump in the waves, let's splash and let's play,
Forget all our worries, just laugh the day away.
For in this grand ocean, with giggles on shore,
Every wave brings a joke, let's laugh even more!

Unveiling Neptune's Stories

Neptune sits back with a big, goofy grin,
Telling tall tales of where he's been.
With mermaids and mermen all clapping their fins,
As he spins wild yarns about oceanic sins.

"I once rode a whale through a shark's wild parade,
And slipped on a sea cucumber, what a cascade!
The octopus laughed, but I made him my friend,
We juggled some pearls 'til the night started to end."

The seahorses burst with laughter and cheer,
As Neptune declares, "I've no worries here!"
He challenges waves to a wrestling match,
While the clams place bets on the next wave to catch.

So raise up a shell and toast to the sea,
Where stories are plenty and wild as can be.
Life in the deep is a marvelous game,
And Neptune, the joker, is never to blame!

Beneath the Surface, a Tale Awaits

Beneath the waves lies a world full of quirks,
Where jellyfish boogie and sea cucumbers lurk.
A turtle named Lou had a shell made of cheese,
And swam with his buddies with absolute ease.

The fish organized races, with fins fully charged,
While crabs took the lead, waving flags like a charge.
But Lou just floated, with his snack at the ready,
As the bottom-dwellers cheered, 'Lou, keep it steady!'

Anemones giggled, tickling fish that swam by,
As clams took selfies, saying "Oh my, oh my!"
Each drift of the current brought laughter and jive,
In this underwater world, everyone's alive.

So dive into fun, let the bubbles surround,
The silliness echoes in the oceanic sound.
For beneath all the waves, in the blue tide's embrace,
A tale swims forever, full of laughter and grace!

Oceanic Dreams Under Starlit Skies

Beneath the stars, the seashells come out,
With fish throwing raves and dancing about.
The moon plays DJ, spinning tunes oh so bright,
While the tide keeps the beat on this magical night.

A whale named Wally had dreams of his own,
To sing to the world from the depths of his throne.
But his voice was more like a foghorn's loud blare,
Yet the fish flopped along, not a single one cared.

Stars flicker above as the waves gently sway,
While crabs pull pranks, claiming they 'made' the bay.
An octopus juggles, but drops all his balls,
Yet laughter erupts through the oceanic halls.

So come join the fun beneath sparkling skies,
With laughter and joy where the seashells all rise.
For under this blanket of stars shining bright,
We dream of a world where all giggles take flight!

Ghosts of the Briny Depths

In the depths, fish wear hats,
Pretending to be cool cats.
Ghosts play cards in the seaweed,
Betting on sea cucumber greed.

Crabs tap dance on the sandy floor,
While octopuses pretend to roar.
With bubbles and giggles, they schemed,
A party planned, or so it seemed.

Clams cracking jokes, oh what a sight,
Making pearls shine in the moonlight.
Eels playing hide and seek so bold,
While jellyfish flash tales unold.

So dive deep where the laughter's abound,
Where even the sharks have fun clowning around.
For under the waves, absurdity reigns,
In the depths where the ocean entertains!

Silent Songs of the Abyss

The fish have formed a choir nice,
Singing tunes of overcooked rice.
A turtle laughs at a sea bass's plight,
As it sings off-key with all its might.

Seahorses dance in a wavy line,
With starfish making faces so fine.
They sway to the tides, such a sight to behold,
While corals gossip, their stories retold.

Anemones tickle the passing crabs,
While seaweed sways, it's all good jabs.
The deep is a stage where the silly convene,
With luminescent fish making a scene.

So listen close to the silent beat,
Of the ocean's jesters, they can't be beat.
For deep down below where the funny reigns,
The songs of the abyss play joyfully unchained!

Lullabies from the Foam

The waves hum soft, a humorous tune,
As barnacles dance beneath the moon.
Seashells chime like tiny bells,
While crabs whisper their shuffling spells.

A dolphin sneezes, a ripple it sends,
A shark plays fetch, with its fishy friends.
The tide whispers jokes to kelp and sand,
In this bubble of laughter, all is quite grand.

Sleep now, dear fish, the foam's your bed,
Where silly dreams float above your head.
Octopuses juggle and sea turtles snore,
While plankton giggle, longing for more.

In these waves of delight, slumber awaits,
With laughter and dancing, all is first rates.
So drift off sweetly, let the fun roam,
For the ocean sings lullabies, cheerful as foam!

Breath of the Wind and Water

The breezes tickle the sea, oh so bright,
While fish tell tales that give quite a fright.
A friendly whale mimics a saxophone,
As seagulls join in, making it known.

Waves tumble over with giggles and glee,
As crusty old crabs sip their minty tea.
What a ruckus beneath the sun's glow,
As antics unfold in the ocean below.

The winds play tag with the frothy tide,
And sea stars wink as they try to hide.
It's a carnival feel on this watery stage,
Where even the plankton join in the page.

Join the fun where the sea meets the sky,
With each giggle and burble, you can't help but sigh.
For this dance of the water and whimsical air,
Brings laughter and joy beyond compare!

Salted Serenades

The seagulls squawk with glee,
While crabs do the cha-cha on the sand,
Fish are laughing at the spree,
In this saltiest wonderland.

Wave after wave, they dance with flair,
A coral conga line, so spry,
Shells spin out in a maritime air,
As the tide joins in, oh my!

The clownfish dons a tiny hat,
While starfish pose in balmy rays,
Octopuses juggle with a spat,
And mermaids sing in silly ways.

So raise a glass to ocean's jest,
Where laughter bubbles from the deep,
In this watery world, we're blessed,
With giggles that never sleep.

Currents of Forgotten Tales

The tide brings stories, in waves they flock,
Of pirates who danced with jellyfish,
Mermaids who played hopscotch on rocks,
And dolphins who dream of becoming swish.

Old bottles float, with messages bold,
Of romances with barnacles and sea foam,
Each tide a tale, not quite gold,
More like nonsense, from oceans' home.

Seahorses, they gossip, tails entwined,
Whispering secrets of deep azure,
About a fish who lost his mind,
In search of a treasure, so obscure.

So listen close to the currents' song,
For laughter's hidden in their tales,
In every bubble where we belong,
The ocean's heart, playfully pales.

The Language of the Sea

With a splash and a crash, the ocean gabbles,
Shells gossip like old ladies in the sun,
Starfish tell jokes that leave us in stables,
And waves high-five just for fun.

Turtles get caught in the bubble speak,
As seaweed tries to weave a yarn,
They laugh and roll, while currents sneak,
Through underwater realms, with charm.

The clams store humor, locked tight in shells,
While jellyfish float, floating in bliss,
Making folks giggle, in quick short spells,
With every wave, a humorous kiss.

So dive right in, hear the ocean's cheer,
Join in the laugh, no need to be shy,
In the dance of salt, we find all so dear,
And with each laugh, together we fly.

Beneath the Blue Veil

Beneath the waves where fishy dwell,
Anemones tease, 'Come join the fun!'
Where sea cucumbers spin and sell,
Their shimmery smiles, a brightened run.

Whales sing off-key, what a strange show,
As plankton raves in a tiny ball,
Giggling currents, where silliness grows,
Making jellyfish do the vertical crawl.

Coral reefs murmur, 'Don't take it too hard',
They throw a party with shells and foam,
As creatures all gather, oh, they'll not discard,
This playful bash, they call their home.

So come take a dip in this jovial spree,
Where underwater antics will surely delight,
With laughter and joy, as far as you see,
Beneath the blue veil, the feelings ignite.

Stories Embodied in Shells

Shells on the sand, so bright and bold,
Each one a story, waiting to be told.
A crab in a shell, with a gown that's all wrong,
Says, "Fashion's a tide, it can change with the song."

A starfish with glasses, staring at the waves,
Claims he's the smartest; he knows all the raves.
But when he waves back, it's a total faux pas,
Said he's just shy, not a star of the spa!

A clam joins the dance, a wild little thing,
Says, "Life's just a party when you're under the bling!"
But just when he twirls, he flips right and wrong,
Yells, "Help! I'm caught in this shell-bopping song!"

So tiptoe on shores where the critters do play,
And listen for laughter—it's never far away.
Where shells spin their tales in a comical way,
And the ocean's a stage for a grand cabaret!

The Silence Between the Swells

When the waves take a pause, and the sea seems quite still,
Crabs practice their waltz on the edge of a hill.
The dolphins, they giggle, in synchronized glee,
As seagulls look down, screaming, "Look at me!"

A fish in a tux, just trying to impress,
Says, "I'm quite dapper, don't you think I'm the best?"
But as he spins round, he gets caught in some seaweed,
Choking on glam, he keeps missing the beat!

The mermaids, they pause, with swimming to do,
To laugh at the fish in his awkward debut.
They toss sea cucumbers, all in the jest,
As deep as a scoop of their diva-like quest.

So savor those moments when water is calm,
For giggles and gaggles release all the qualm.
The sea sings a tune, just a tickle and tease,
In the silence between waves, anything can please!

Secrets in the Coral's Embrace

In the corals so bright, where the fish love to hide,
A clownfish named Charlie thinks he's quite a guide.
He tells all the young ones, "Life's grand and it's swell,
Just avoid the octopus; he's not a sweet sell!"

A parrotfish chuckles, with colors that flash,
"Worry not about style; I'll just eat the trash!"
He feasts on the scraps that the others could stash,
Sings about eco-friends, making a splash.

Coral reefs giggle, their branches like arms,
Inviting all critters with curious charms.
A shrimp in a tutu does flips in delight,
Looks up at the moon and says, "What a night!"

So wander the reefs where the secrets run deep,
In laughter and colors, the ocean does leap.
Embrace all the sillies that swim hand in hand,
For in coral's sweet hold, we find joy at hand!

Shadows in the Deep

In the deep where it's dark, shadows wiggle and creep,
A ghostly old squid can't quite take a leap.
He's boasting of treasures, a chest full of gold,
But really it's just where his snacks are controlled.

A pufferfish shimmies, all swollen with pride,
Claims he's got secrets; just look at his hide!
But when he tries to share, he just puffs up with fear,
And laughs at his antics, "I'm more drink than beer!"

A sea turtle grins, while drifting along,
"Mistakes are what make us," he sings to a song.
He's wearing a hat made of lost fishing line,
Says, "Fashion is fluid; I'm here to enshrine!"

So wander with shadows in the depths of the blue,
Where laughter is hidden, waiting to ensue.
In the depths of the ocean, don't take it too deep,
For humor is waiting, in shadows that leap!

Secrets of the Wind-Kissed Water

The fish gossip, swirling in schools,
While crabs dance like they've lost their rules.
Starfish play poker, with jellyfish bets,
Each splash is a secret that nobody gets.

Seagulls squawk tales of the last big catch,
While dolphins giggle, plotting their match.
In this watery world, joy never lacks,
As sea turtles ride on the ocean's backs.

Pufferfish puffing, they think they're tough,
But a gentle wave says, 'That's quite enough!'
Their jokes float between the foam and the spray,
In this wild aquatic cabaret.

So if you listen, in the tide's soft hum,
You'll hear the laughter of the ocean's drum.
Secrets carried on briny breeze,
Where every ripple brings smiles, if you please.

Serenity in the Melody of Gulls

Gulls take flight, with a comical flair,
They squabble for snacks, without a care.
One swoops down, and the others take chase,
A feathery ballet, a hilarious race.

They squawk at the sun, complain of the heat,
While pelicans ponder their next fishy treat.
With flappy wings, they practice their jokes,
In the theater of tides, where humor evokes.

Murmurs of waves blend with cawing delight,
As seabirds spin tales in the day and the night.
They poke fun at boats, with sails billowed wide,
As sailors roll their eyes, trying not to chide.

In this serenade where laughter's the call,
The gulls stand united, ready to brawl.
So join in their glee, let your troubles take flight,
As the melodies soar, and the world feels right.

The Clamor of the Stormy Seas

When waves crash loud, like a toddler's shout,
Seas get melodramatic, there's no doubt.
They throw a fit, tossing boats with glee,
While sailors cling tight, like a dog to a tree.

Lightning zaps, and the thunder replies,
As fish hide in shells, rolling their eyes.
It's a soap opera, with barnacles cast,
While plankton yell out, 'This storm won't last!'

Clouds in a panic, they storm the scene,
With winds blowing wildly, and skies turning green.
But somewhere beneath, the clownfish all cheer,
As the chaos above brings a grin from ear to ear.

So let's laugh at the tempest, not shed a tear,
For the wild sea's show is something to cheer.
Just hold your hat tight, in the ocean's loud scream,
And ride out the storm, with a splash and a dream.

Untold Histories in the Sand

Footprints abound, in a curious line,
'Was it the crab or a bird?' they opine.
Shells tell tales of a beachside ball,
Where sandcastles conquered, but crumbled in fall.

Each grain a memory, a story untold,
Of creatures who mingled, both brave and bold.
The seaweed debates what it's heard at night,
As the tide rolls in, sharing giggles and fright.

Starfish recount soothing maritime dreams,
As clams hide their laughs, plotting regal schemes.
The tide pool is bustling, with gossip so grand,
In this jokester's realm of the sun-kissed sand.

So next time you wander along the shore,
Listen closely to tales, and you'll find even more.
For history giggles in each ocean breeze,
A comedy sketch, if you just pause with ease.

Murmurs Beneath the Lighthouse

The waves giggle like kids at play,
As seagulls steal fries, laughing all day.
The lighthouse winks, a cheeky old chap,
While crabs in the sand take a nap and a nap.

The tide pulls in jokes from the salty breeze,
A clam sings softly, like it's trying to tease.
Fish tell tall tales in fins of bright hues,
While starfish wear shades, sipping on blues.

The buoys bounce around, dancing with glee,
While jellyfish float, oh so carelessly.
The boats wave their sails, gossip on the run,
Life on the coast is just too much fun!

So hear the sea's laughter, a youthful delight,
A melody wrapped in the warm ocean light.
Let the waves tickle your toes in the foam,
In this lively seaside, we find our sweet home.

Dreams Woven in Seaweed

Seaweed's a blanket, tangled and tight,
It whispers to fish as they swim out of sight.
With dreams woven in kelp right under the sun,
Octopuses giggle, 'Oh, what a fun run!'

The crabs in the rocks throw a stylish soirée,
With fireworks of bubbles that dance and sway.
A dolphin provides tunes on its slick back,
While clams tap their shells to the rhythmic clack.

Sea stars make wishes on waves made of dreams,
While mollusks engage in their science memes.
The ocean's a playhouse, a raucous retreat,
Where every creature has chances to meet!

So laugh with the sea, embrace its delight,
With dreams in the waves and stars shining bright.
Join the parade of the salty parade,
In this whimsical world where laughter is made.

The Language of Driftwood

Driftwood is chatting on the warm sand,
It talks of adventures, both funny and grand.
With knots in its bark and stories to weave,
This wood from the sea has tricks up its sleeve.

The tides bring it gossip, like old fishing lore,
As shells listen close, begging for more.
Anchors drop puns, and the sea turtles chuckle,
While shoals of bright fish all circle and snuggle.

Old nets tell of tales, oh, the things they have caught,
While sea urchins snicker at the wisdom they sought.
A pelican poised, with its beak held up high,
Joins in the humor, oh my, oh my!

So gather the laughter from the wood and the tide,
In the chorus of creatures, there's nothing to hide.
With driftwood as a guide, let your spirit be bright,
Explore delights hidden in the ocean's pure light.

Odes to the Celestial Tide

The moon plays tricks with the pull of the sea,
It bends and it stretches, a big tease, whee!
Stars twinkle bright, like they're laughing above,
While waves roll in, with a giggle and shove.

A lobster in slippers leads the sandy charge,
To dance with the shells in a mermaid's barge.
Sea foam collects jokes from the winds far away,
And dolphins burst forth in a splashy ballet.

Barnacles crack up at the ship's heavy load,
While tidal pools shimmer with laughter bestowed.
The breezes come whispering tales old and new,
In this world of delight, the laughter rings true.

So take a deep breath of that salty breeze,
Join in the fun with the jellyfish squeeze.
With odes to the tide and its whimsical ride,
Let's dance on the shore where the joyful reside.

The Heartbeat of Mariner's Legends

Old sailors tell tales so wild,
Of fish that dance and mermaids styled.
But with every swig of rum they take,
Their stories get stranger, make no mistake.

With nets made of spaghetti, quite funny!
They fish for laughs, not fresh crab or honey.
One claims he caught a whale so big,
But really it was just his pet pig!

In every port, they spin the yarns,
Of storms they conquered, of hidden barns.
But in their hearts, they hold a stash,
Of goofy times and a friendly bash.

So raise a glass to the mariner clan,
Where laughter flows, and jokes can span.
For every tale that'll make you grin,
Is just the storm where their fun begins!

Sighs of the Surf

Oh, the waves, they giggle and play,
Splashing silliness in a frothy display.
They say the tide has jokes untold,
Like why crabs never share their gold!

The seagulls gossip, flap their wings,
About fishy love and underwater flings.
With every squawk, the tales get weirder,
But the ocean's laughter makes them cheerier!

An octopus rolls its eyes with a sigh,
As jellyfish waltz, floating so high.
They bubble and chuckle, causing quite a scene,
While turtle sunbathes, looking serene!

So listen close when the sea takes a breath,
It's more than fun; it's a life in jest.
In each wave's caress is a joke to find,
A treasure of laughter for those so inclined!

Treasures in the Tide

Digging in sand for lost riches bright,
But all they find are a crab's silly bites.
The treasures of pain, they all wear a grin,
As seaweed wigs their little fish kin.

They search for pearls, but what's their prize?
Just flip-flops and shells and a surprise.
A goldfish wearing sunglasses on parade,
In the tide's laughter, their worries fade!

Each bucket they haul, filled with glee,
Holds shrimp that dance, surf fish on spree.
Shells sing harmonies, beachballs speak,
In this quirky realm, it's laughter we seek!

So here's to the beachcombers and fun,
Whose treasure is joy, and that's just the run.
For in every tide pool, the silliness flows,
More golden than gold, everybody knows!

Forgotten Echoes

In caves of the coast, jokes echo around,
Of clams with no sense, lost but not found.
They giggle in whispers, behind rocky walls,
As waves crash in laughter, like bounce from their falls.

Forgotten echoes of fishy banter,
With dolphins who moonwalk, they sure know how to canter.
They slide on the waves, in rhythm, they flow,
While crabs tell tall tales of the sea below.

But in quiet moments, the fish take a pause,
Pointing at gophers, now holding applause.
And as the tide rolls, the stories swirl,
While off in the distance, a pelican twirls.

Remember these echoes, for when the tide's low,
The humor still bubbles, ready to show.
In whispers and giggles, the sea's silly heart,
Will forever echo, it's a true work of art!

Harmonies of Sand and Sea

The seagulls squawk a silly tune,
While crabs dance in the afternoon.
Sandcastles tilt and start to sway,
As waves sneak in to steal the day.

Kids chase tides, then trip and fall,
Splashing water, laughing loud, all.
A beach ball flies, oh what a sight,
As sunscreen battles sun so bright.

The seaweed wiggles, oh so sly,
Tickling toes as fish swim by.
Starfish wear their grins with pride,
Taking naps where they can hide.

So let us dance 'neath sun so bold,
With shells that jingle, stories told.
The ocean's laughter fills the air,
In this wild game of beach affair.

Soul of the Forgotten Harbor

A lighthouse winks, its bulb so bright,
  As boats get lost in vain delight.
 The tide's a trickster, pulling pranks,
  While dolphins giggle in the banks.

 Forgotten nets reclaim the shore,
  Fish play poker, what a score!
 Barnacles laugh on rusty beams,
While seagulls plot their silly schemes.

 Old buoys bob like happy cheer,
  Each splash a song, a joke to hear.
 The gulls share tales of lost old shoes,
  As waves hum softly, sharing news.

 In mellow light, the harbor glows,
  As all the ocean's mischief flows.
So here's to laughter, waves, and glee,
  In this place of secrets by the sea.

Embrace of the Gentle Swells

The waves come in with silly sighs,
Tickling toes and slipping ties.
Surfboards wobble, losing grace,
As surfers tumble in the race.

A fish darts past, wearing a hat,
Who knew they'd give it such a spat?
The sea spouts bubbles, oh what joy,
As crabs march by, a mini army boy.

Seashells chatter, each with a tale,
Of sandy mishaps and a fishy sale.
The beachcomber hides behind his shades,
While chasing jellies in funny parades.

So let us play where tides unfold,
In waves of laughter, bright and bold.
With sun on skin and pebbles free,
We'll share our giggles with the sea.

Resonance of Shells on the Shore

The shells all sing in harmony,
A conch plays lounge for all to see.
Hermit crabs strut in fancy shoes,
As beachgoers dive for ocean's blues.

Each wave a joke, a splashy jest,
With jellyfish wearing a silly vest.
The sunbathers snooze, while kids embark,
To build a home for gloves and bark.

The tides will tease and then retreat,
While starfish giggle in the heat.
Sand dollars count their treasure hoard,
As pelicans dive and strike the chords.

So gather 'round the sea's embrace,
Where humor dances, brings a smile to your face.
Let the shells join in this joyful song,
In the land where sandy dreams belong.

The Call of the Endless Blue

The fish all gathered 'round for games,
Debating who had the silliest names.
One claimed he swam like a dolphin's brother,
But really, he just floated like no other.

The crab cracked jokes with a pinch and a jest,
While the seaweed groaned, 'I need some rest!'
A jellyfish wobbled, saying with a grin,
'At least I'm not stuck in a plastic bin!'

The sea turtles surfed on a bubbly wave,
While starfish danced, giving the barnacles a rave.
'Why don't we create a splashy new trend?'
They laughed and spun, 'Who knew fish could bend?'

So under the sun, they laughed with glee,
A raucous party beneath the sea.
With bubbles and giggles, they swirled about,
Their ocean antics made everyone shout!

A Dance of Dolphins at Dusk

A pod of dolphins leaped for fun,
Practicing flips as the day was done.
One tried a twist, but oh, what a flop,
And landed with splashes—a belly flop stop!

With squeaks and clicks, they called it a show,
Challenging each other, 'Come on, let's go!'
The seagulls chuckled from high in the sky,
'You'd never get a medal; not even a pie!'

They danced through the waves, so slick and spry,
One dolphin shouted, 'Who needs to fly?'
The fish all snickered, a bubbly delight,
As fins flailed wildly in the fading light.

So when you hear laughter near the shore,
Know the dolphins are up to fun, for sure!
With silly moves in the setting sun,
They left their splashy dance, oh what a run!

Moonlit Whispers Upon the Waves

Beneath the moonshine, a tide made of glee,
The crabs threw a party by the edge of the sea.
They brought out the snacks—seashells piled high,
And whispered their secrets to the nearby fry.

A clownfish juggled like a pro with a shell,
While an octopus gave magic tricks a swell.
'Though my arms are long, I can't catch a break,
Just look at my dance—it's a big fishy flake!'

They twirled and they swayed, under the night's embrace,

With starry companions watching their chase.
The shrimp stuck around for the laughter and fun,
As barnacles whispered, 'A seaweed bun!'

So if you stroll by when the night's feeling bright,
Listen for echoes of joyous delight.
For under the waves where the silver rays play,
The ocean's wild tales are a splashy ballet!

Harmony in the Splashing Surf

At dawn in the surf, the surfboards did race,
While seagulls swooped down, a comical chase.
One surfer yelled, 'Hey, I'm the king of the wave!'
But tripped on a clam, oh how he misbehaved!

The seals all applauded with flippers held high,
While the fish rolled their eyes, 'Oh me, oh my!'
A whale splashed water in a grand salute,
'Next time, try dodging that slippery brute!'

Then came the tide, with a splash and a roll,
Where laughter echoed, everybody stole,
The beachball's quite bouncy, but one gained a frown,
'That's not invited!' said the log, feeling brown!

And as the sun dipped, the antics grew bold,
With sea stars clapping, their memories told.
So if you come near with a smile full of cheer,
Join the splashy party, the fun is all here!

www.ingramcontent.com/pod-product-compliance
Lightning Source LLC
Chambersburg PA
CBHW072135070526
44585CB00016B/1686